Secrets Cradled in Twilight

In twilight's hush, whispers loom,
Soft sighs weave through the gloom.
Dreams flicker in fading light,
Holding secrets, hidden from sight.

Stars awake, blink and glance,
Dancing shadows in a trance.
Ancient tales the night will keep,
In twilight's arms, mysteries sleep.

Echoes of Forgotten Legends

Beneath the ancient, twisted trees,
Voices drift upon the breeze.
Echoes rise from the silent stone,
Stories of heroes long overthrown.

Time weaves tales in twilight's fold,
Legends whispered, brave and bold.
Footsteps fade down cobbled ways,
Remnants of long-lost days.

The Unspoken Code of the Cosmos

Stars align in silent grace,
Every glimmer holds a trace.
In the vastness, secrets dwell,
Written deep in a cosmic shell.

Galaxies spin, tales untold,
In the darkness, truths unfold.
Celestial whispers guide the heart,
In this dance, we play our part.

Nebulous Questions in the Dark

In shadows deep, questions rise,
Flickering like distant fires.
What lies beyond the shimmering veil?
Does the cosmos hold our tale?

Each twinkle spins a fresh debate,
Life's mysteries eluding fate.
In the dark, we seek the light,
Nebulous dreams take flight.

The Conundrum of Cosmic Patterns

In the vastness of the night, they dwell,
Stars entwined in secrets to tell.
Galaxies spin in a harmonious dance,
Each twinkle a question, a cosmic romance.

Mysteries woven in the fabric of space,
Infinite wonders we dare to embrace.
Patterns that shift, yet always remain,
Whispers of truth in the shadow of pain.

Time as a river, forever it flows,
Carrying dreams where the starlight glows.
In the silence, a voice softly calls,
Chasing the echoes through celestial halls.

Lurking in the Astral Abyss

Deep in the void, shadows entwine,
Where dreams and nightmares both align.
Stars flicker like ghosts in forgotten lore,
Haunting the silence forevermore.

A cosmic dance in the nebulous sway,
Where light bends and colors decay.
Eclipsed by the dark, secrets unfold,
Tales of the ancients in whispers told.

Echoes of silence fill the vast night,
Lurking amongst the fading light.
A curtain of stars, shimmering and bright,
Concealing the depths of the astral plight.

Tales Whispers on the Wind

Stories carried on a gentle breeze,
Softly they flutter through the swaying trees.
Echoes of laughter, shadows of tears,
Whispers of love transcending the years.

From mountain peaks to the valley floor,
The wind holds the tales of those before.
In every rustle, a memory clings,
Carried along on the breath of wings.

Fables of heartache, joy, and despair,
Intertwined softly in the cool, crisp air.
Listen closely, for what it may send,
Are fragments of life that never quite end.

The Twilight Chronicles

In shadows deep, where whispers blur,
The twilight dances, as night's warm fur.
A tale unfolds, both vast and small,
In twilight's grasp, we heed the call.

With echoes soft, the stars ignite,
Their flicker guides us through the night.
Each step we take, a story spun,
The twilight chronicles have begun.

Secrets in the Celestial Sea

Beneath the waves of starlit dreams,
The cosmic tide flows, or so it seems.
Secrets hidden in depths so wide,
In the celestial sea, we must confide.

Waves of time, they ebb and flow,
Carrying tales from long ago.
In the shimmer of light, we find our way,
Through the secrets of night and day.

A Journey to the Ether's Edge

Beyond the skies, where angels tread,
In realms unknown, we dare to head.
The ether calls with a gentle hand,
Inviting us to a distant land.

With every breath, our spirits soar,
Unlocking doors to forevermore.
On ethereal paths, we boldly stride,
A journey awaits, with stars as guide.

The Wandering Star's Tale

A star adrift in the velvet night,
Chasing echoes of distant light.
With dreams so grand, it roams the sky,
The wandering star, where wishes fly.

In every twinkle, stories arise,
Of secret realms and timeless skies.
Through cosmic fields, it weaves and spins,
The wandering star, where magic begins.

Secrets Beyond the Cloud

Whispers float on gentle breeze,
Hidden truths are hard to seize.
Veiled in light, the shadows play,
Secrets kept till end of day.

Beneath the sky, the stories tell,
Of dreams that in silence dwell.
Each heartbeat wears a muted cloak,
In twilight's grip, their magic spoke.

Glimmers dance on silver streams,
Carrying forth our silent dreams.
Eclipsed by stars that fade away,
The secrets linger, come what may.

Luminous Echoes at Dusk

In twilight's blush, the echoes hum,
Each shadow whispers, soft and numb.
The sun dips low, a golden sigh,
Waves of light that gently die.

Silhouettes against the fading sky,
Where day meets night, we can't deny.
Each star emerges, bold and bright,
As echoes shatter the veil of night.

Colors merge in sweet embrace,
In this soft, enchanted space.
Time unwinds in a delicate tune,
With echoes resonating like a croon.

The Language of Starlit Silence

In stillness deep, the cosmos breathes,
Each star a note that softly weaves.
Hushed whispers in the void so clear,
Speak the truths we long to hear.

The moonlight spills its silver grace,
In shadowed night, we find our place.
Silent stories carried far,
Each twinkling light, a hidden scar.

Constellations form a timeless bond,
In starlit silence, we respond.
A gentle pulse of cosmic dreams,
Awakening hope in quiet streams.

Enigmas Above the Horizon

Beyond the hills, the secrets lie,
Wrapped in whispers of the sky.
A dance of clouds, a fleeting form,
Beckoning forth the silent storm.

Each sunset paints an unseen tale,
Where shadows mingle and dreams sail.
The horizon, a canvas wide,
Holds enigmas in constant glide.

With every dawn, new mysteries rise,
A tapestry of endless skies.
We seek the truth in every hue,
In each soft breath, starts anew.

Celestial Riddles in the Firmament

Stars blink softly in the night,
Secrets hidden, pure delight.
Constellations weave their tales,
Guiding ships with starlit sails.

Planets dance in silent grace,
Each a story, each a place.
Galaxies swirl, patterns unfold,
Mysteries waiting to be told.

Comets streak across the sky,
Carrying wishes as they fly.
Nebulas bloom in colors bright,
Painting dreams in ethereal light.

In the vastness, questions rise,
What lies beyond our earthly skies?
In the firmament, echoes call,
Celestial riddles, they enthrall.

The Unseen Guardians Above

In the shadows, watchful eyes,
Silent sentinels from the skies.
Moonbeams glow with gentle light,
Guardians watch through the night.

Whispers carried on the breeze,
Tales of hope among the trees.
Stars will guide the lost and strayed,
Angels linger, unafraid.

Constellations form a shield,
In their light, hearts never yield.
Each twinkling spark a sign of grace,
Lighting paths in empty space.

Through dark times, they abide,
A celestial force, a cosmic tide.
With every dawn, they rise anew,
The unseen guardians, always true.

Stellar Whispers in the Wind

In the hush of twilight's veil,
Stellar whispers softly sail.
Carried on the softest breeze,
Echoes dance among the trees.

Night unveils its velvet cloak,
Stars converse, a gentle yoke.
Each twinkle shares a secret tune,
Sung beneath the watchful moon.

Galaxies murmur, ancient rhymes,
Telling tales of distant times.
Listen close, let silence mend,
Stellar whispers, time's old friend.

Hearts attune to cosmic sighs,
In their depth, the universe lies.
Through the night, our spirits blend,
In the wind, the stars ascend.

The Enchantress of Aurora's Glow

In twilight's grasp, she starts to weave,
Colors dance, and hearts believe.
The enchantress in her luminous shroud,
Whispers secrets, soft yet loud.

Crimson, violet, emerald hues,
Light the canvas with magical views.
As she twirls in the frigid skies,
Hope ignites in dreamers' eyes.

Each wave a brushstroke, bold and free,
Painting wonders for all to see.
In her glow, the night takes flight,
An enchantress, a beacon of light.

So gaze upon her fleeting art,
Let her beauty warm your heart.
For in the northern lights' embrace,
Lives the magic of endless grace.

Enchanted Stars and Moonbeams

In the night, dreams take flight,
Glowing softly, a gentle light.
Whispers of hopes in the skies,
Dancing beams, where magic lies.

Underneath the velvet dome,
Every star becomes our home.
Guiding hearts with their soft glow,
Through the night, love's rivers flow.

Navigating the Ethereal Canvas

Stars like gems on fabric spun,
Each unique, a tale begun.
Painting skies in vibrant hues,
Navigating the cosmic cues.

Guided by the moon's embrace,
Charting paths in endless space.
In the silence, secrets speak,
Infinite dreams, so bold yet meek.

Cloaked Wonders Above

Cloaked in midnight's tender veil,
Wonders weave a silent tale.
Constellations, ancient lore,
Whispered myths from days of yore.

Glimmers in the darkened night,
Sparkling threads of pure delight.
Cloaked in shadows, bright and dim,
Chasing dreams, on hope we swim.

Celestial Signposts of Wonder

Celestial signposts guide the way,
In the night, they brightly sway.
Marking journeys, hearts aligned,
In their shine, peace we find.

Wonders woven through each star,
Tales of loved ones from afar.
In their glow, we walk the line,
Celestial whispers, love divine.

Starlit Riddles

In the night where shadows blend,
Whispers of the cosmos send.
A tapestry of sparkles bright,
Guarding secrets in the light.

Questions dance on silver beams,
Unraveling the midnight dreams.
Silent answers, soft and clear,
Echo through the atmosphere.

Each bright star a tale untold,
Mysteries of the brave and bold.
In stillness, wisdom finds its place,
Embraced by the vastness of space.

Starlit riddles call to me,
In the dark, I long to see.
A universe so deep and wide,
Where wonders and truths abide.

In the Realm of Nebulae

Hidden worlds beyond the veil,
Glimmers where the starlings sail.
Colors swirl in cosmic dance,
Fractions of an endless trance.

Silken threads of fiery light,
Weave the fabric of the night.
In the nebulae's embrace,
Time and space begin to race.

Mysterious births and deaths collide,
In this realm where dreams reside.
Stars are born from dust and sighs,
In the cradle where stardust lies.

Floating softly, silent grace,
Melodies of the endless space.
In the realm where wonders play,
Nebulae hold the night at bay.

Constellations' Silent Secrets

In the heavens, patterns glow,
Stories only starlight knows.
Shapes of lore and ancient lore,
Whispered soft on celestial shore.

Beneath the arch of night so vast,
Memories of the future cast.
Constellations weave and thread,
Silent secrets long since shed.

Bearing witness to our plight,
Guiding through the darkest night.
Each formation, silent song,
Tells of where we all belong.

Constellations watch and wait,
Guarding tales of love and fate.
In their silence, truths unfold,
Secrets written, never told.

Flight of the Cosmic Ravens

On the wings of midnight skies,
Ravens soar where starlight flies.
Shadows shifting through the night,
Carrying whispers of the light.

Feathers woven of the dark,
Each a tale, a hidden spark.
Eyes like embers, keen and bright,
Tracing paths of cosmic flight.

Through the void, their cries resound,
Echoes lost but never found.
They navigate the astral maze,
Dancing in the silver haze.

In their flight, a story spins,
Of beginnings, ends, and wins.
Cosmic ravens, bold and free,
Guardians of eternity.

Eclipsed Revelations

In shadows deep where secrets blend,
A whisper rides on twilight's end.
Stars flicker softly, a silent call,
Revealing truths that hide from all.

Through veils of night, a journey starts,
Unraveling tales entwined in hearts.
The moonlight dances, shy and bold,
As stories of the past unfold.

Reflections glimmer on a quiet lake,
Echoes of choices we dare to make.
Each ripple carries a dream unmet,
In the embrace of cosmic debt.

Awakened souls in twilight's glow,
Gathering wisdom only they know.
In eclipsed moments, life stands still,
Revelations whispering, time to chill.

Journeys Beyond the Stratosphere

Up high where the eagles dare to fly,
Beyond the clouds, where dreams drift by.
A realm where stars weave paths so bright,
And wonders bloom in the soft starlight.

Rocketing forth on cosmic streams,
In search of worlds birthed from our dreams.
Gravity fades, liberation sings,
As we embrace what the sky brings.

Galaxies swirl in a dance divine,
Each twinkling star, a wish to find.
In silence profound, we chase the light,
Journeys unfurling into the night.

With hearts as wide as the endless sea,
We wander spaces of eternity.
Beyond the stratosphere, we take flight,
Adventurers soaring, hearts alight.

The Language of the Wind

A gentle breath, a soft caress,
Whispers through leaves, a quiet press.
Messages travel from tree to tree,
In every gust, nature's decree.

It sighs in rhythms, a tuneful song,
Echoes of stories that linger long.
Caressing mountains, it dances free,
The wind, a poet, wild and free.

In fleeting moments, it calls our name,
Each breeze a whisper, never the same.
Secrets of ages twirl like leaves,
In the language of wind, the heart believes.

Through valleys deep and hills so high,
It speaks in silence, no need to cry.
A symphony played on a world so wide,
In the language of the wind, we confide.

Ethereal Patterns of Light

Through prism beams, the colors twine,
An artwork painted, pure and fine.
Dancing shadows on the wall,
Ethereal patterns, a visual thrall.

Sunrise whispers, dusk deepens desires,
Each ray of light, the heart conspires.
In every angle, life takes flight,
Weaving tales in the fabric of light.

Dreams reflected upon the sea,
Waves glisten softly, wild and free.
Mosaic fragments of a day gone by,
In the spectrum's embrace, we learn to fly.

Fleeting moments, forever caught,
In the dance of brilliance, we are taught.
Ethereal patterns that gleam and shift,
A reminder of life's precious gift.

Celestial Cartography

Stars trace paths in velvet skies,
Planets dance through cosmic sighs.
Galaxies whisper to the tune,
Mapping stories in the moonlight's bloom.

Constellations draw a painter's brush,
In astral quiet, dreams are lush.
Navigating night with silent grace,
Celestial maps in time and space.

Shooting stars arc through the dark,
Each a wish, a fleeting spark.
In the vastness, tales unfold,
Of ancient dreams yet to be told.

Veils of Celestial Dreams

In twilight's grasp, the heavens sigh,
A tapestry of dreams drawn nigh.
Veils of light in shades of blue,
Whisper secrets in the dew.

Comets blaze with fiery trails,
Carrying hopes on cosmic sails.
In the stillness, the heart gleams,
Chasing shadows of celestial dreams.

Nebulas cradle starlit sighs,
Painting beauty across vast skies.
In nocturnal wonder, hearts align,
Veils of dreams in cosmic design.

Whispers in the Night's Embrace

The night unfolds her velvet grace,
With whispers soft, a warm embrace.
Moonlight spills like silver rain,
Filling hearts with sweet refrain.

Crickets sing their lullabies,
Underneath the starlit skies.
Every shadow holds a story,
Embraced in night's celestial glory.

Echoes dance through silent trees,
Carried gently by the breeze.
Whispers of dreams dwell in the light,
Creating magic in the night.

Shadows of the Moonlit Realm

In the realm where shadows play,
Moonlight weaves a silver ray.
Through the woods, soft footsteps tread,
Echoes of the dreams we've shed.

Melodies of the night unfold,
In whispered tales, both shy and bold.
A dance of leaves, a ghostly sight,
Shadows swirl beneath the light.

Mysterious paths, the heart's delight,
Crimson blooms in the pale twilight.
In the moonlit hush, we find our way,
To the dreams that softly sway.

Illuminated Illusions of Night

Whispers of shadows dance and sway,
In moonlit glow, they gently play.
Secrets linger, softly unfurled,
A dreamlike tapestry, night's own world.

Stars above twinkle their bright eyes,
Painting stories across the skies.
Embers of time, flickering light,
Echoes of life in the still of night.

Veils of darkness cradle the day,
As visions of wonder drift away.
Each moment fleeting, a soft sigh,
Illusions whispered, then goodbye.

Yet in this realm where time suspends,
The night reveals what seldom ends.
In silence, truth finds its way through,
Illuminated dreams, forever new.

Constellation Chronicles

Constellations weave their tales of old,
Stories of heroes and legends bold.
Each star a marker, a point in time,
Chronicled echoes in celestial rhyme.

Beneath the vastness, our thoughts take flight,
Mapping the heavens with dreams of light.
Fables whispered on the cool night air,
Infinite wonders, beyond compare.

In the silence, the cosmos breathes deep,
Waking the dreams that the starlight keeps.
Galaxies spin in a dance sublime,
Tracing the rhythms of time after time.

Through cosmic storms and tranquil skies,
Hope finds a place where the heart complies.
In every twinkle, a chance to see,
The chronicles written in infinity.

Beneath the Veil of the Night Sky

Beneath the veil of velvet black,
The world unfolds, no eye to track.
Whispers of night, a gentle sound,
In stillness, peace is truly found.

Moonbeams drape the earth in light,
Guiding lost souls through the night.
With each star, a wish is cast,
Hopes woven tight, held steadfast.

The silence cradles every dream,
As nature flows like a winding stream.
In shadows deep where spirits dwell,
Mysteries linger, hidden well.

Beneath such splendor, we find our place,
A moment of grace in this vast space.
Each heartbeat echoes in rhythm divine,
As night's gentle whisper becomes our sign.

Celestial Portents and Signs

In twilight's glow, the heavens shift,
Celestial dance, the stars uplift.
Portents flicker, a tale untold,
Signs of destiny in starlit gold.

Comets blaze with a fiery trail,
Marking the paths where dreams set sail.
Orbs of light, in alignment they play,
Guiding our wishes, come what may.

Each constellation a guardian wise,
Holding the secrets of ancient skies.
In their embrace, we seek our fate,
Unraveling mysteries, no longer late.

As night descends, we stand in awe,
Finding our truths in nature's law.
In the vast expanse, our spirits reign,
Celestial signs, our hearts to sustain.

Celestial Queries

Stars whisper secrets in the night,
Planets dance, caught in the light.
Questions rise like vapor trails,
Winding through the cosmic sails.

Comets carve paths through the skies,
Shooting stars grant fleeting sighs.
What lies beyond the endless sphere?
Mysteries, we draw ever near.

Galaxies spin their ancient tales,
In silence, their wonder prevails.
Will we uncover every truth?
Or lose ourselves in timeless youth?

Time and space intertwine and weave,
In their embrace, we dare to believe.
Celestial queries guide our quest,
As we seek the night's behest.

Echoes from the Ether

From the void, a sound takes flight,
Carried softly through the night.
Echoes stir in each still space,
Lingering in time and place.

Voices call from realms unknown,
In every whisper, there's a tone.
An orchestra of distant dreams,
Filling hearts with blazing beams.

Cascading notes like streams of light,
Merging shadows with delight.
What tales do the echoes share?
Through the ether, we find care.

A symphony of lives entwined,
Resonating, souls aligned.
In every pulse, a spark of fate,
Echoes guide us, never late.

The Serpent of the Zenith

High above, the serpent glides,
Curling through the skies it rides.
Scales of silver, gleaming bright,
A harbinger of ancient light.

In the zenith, its spirit coils,
Guarding wisdom that never spoils.
With a hiss, it shares its lore,
Of the heavens and what's in store.

It twists through clouds and stars alike,
A guardian of every spike.
What dreams lie in its endless wake?
The cosmos stirs; the heart can quake.

As day turns dusk and night extends,
The serpent beckons, wisdom blends.
Above, the stories intertwine,
In the dance of fate, divine.

Unraveling the Aurora

Colors swirl in celestial play,
Painting night with a vibrant array.
The aurora whispers, secrets hidden,
In its glow, we feel unbidden.

Dancing lights across the sky,
Twinkling hopes that flutter by.
What truths do these hues unfold?
In the chill, the warmth is bold.

As dawn approaches, shadows wane,
Yet the memory will remain.
Unraveling threads of light and time,
We search for meaning, rhythm, rhyme.

A canvas spun from dreams and lore,
The aurora's heart forevermore.
In each shimmer, we find our place,
Connected through the cosmos' grace.

Shadows Cast by Forgotten Suns

In twilight's embrace, shadows play,
Fading echoes of a bright day.
Whispers of light where dreams once spun,
Now linger softly, shadows run.

Silent figures dance in the dusk,
Memories linger, a fragile husk.
Each moment lost, yet ever near,
In shadows cast, we see our fear.

The warmth of sun, a distant race,
Yet shadows hold their own sweet grace.
In every dark, a hint of light,
From forgotten suns, we chase the night.

So let them stretch, those ghostly lines,
Where time has blended, fate entwines.
For in the depth of night's soft hue,
Shadows reveal what once was true.

Mapping the Uncharted Night

Stars above, a map unspun,
Each flicker tells where dreams begun.
Galaxies swirl in silent flight,
Charting paths through endless night.

Whispers of winds, they weave a tale,
In shadows deep where hopes prevail.
Constellations guide the wandering heart,
In the quiet dark, we play our part.

Night unfolds like a velvet sheet,
Every heartbeat, a rhythmic beat.
In the vast expanse, we lose our way,
Yet find ourselves at break of day.

With courage bold, we chart our course,
Through skies unknown, we feel the force.
In mapping dreams that light the dark,
We find our spark, igniting stark.

Radiant Fragments of Tomorrow

In fragments bright, the future glows,
A tapestry where hope still grows.
Each stitch a dream, so finely spun,
Radiant threads of what's to come.

The dawn shall break, with colors bold,
Stories waiting to be told.
In every hue, a promise laid,
In the light, our fears will fade.

Tomorrow whispers, softly sings,
With every breath, potential springs.
The world awaits with open skies,
In radiant dreams, the heart complies.

So let us chase what lies ahead,
In vibrant hopes, we dare to tread.
For in the fragments of the morn,
The seeds of brilliance are reborn.

The Silent Watchers of the Nocturne

Beneath the moon, the watchers stand,
Guardians of night, a solemn band.
In shadows deep, they keep their oath,
Silent sentinels, none can sloth.

With every star, a tale unfolds,
Ancient secrets, silent holds.
They listen close to the night's soft breath,
In stillness found, they conquer death.

As whispers glide through the midnight air,
The watchers know of dreams and despair.
In hushed repose, they weave their sights,
Anchors of calm in tangled nights.

In every heart, they plant a seed,
Of strength and hope, a gentle creed.
For in the dark, they light the way,
In silent watch, they softly sway.

Celestial Puzzle Pieces

Stars scatter in the night,
Whispers from afar,
Each spark a story bright,
Written in the light.

Galaxies align with grace,
Time's artful embrace,
A cosmic drift we trace,
In this vast space.

Fragments of dreams endure,
Connected, yet obscure,
In the universe, we explore,
Seeking evermore.

Together we find our way,
In constellations' sway,
Celestial puzzle pieces play,
In night's soft ballet.

When Stars Conspire in Silence

Beneath the moon's soft glow,
Stars begin to dance,
In twilight's tender flow,
A celestial romance.

Whispers of wishes shared,
In the quiet night,
Every heart laid bare,
Beneath the starlit light.

Constellations hum a tune,
While shadows softly sway,
As we swoon under the moon,
In time's gentle play.

When stars conspire tonight,
Magic fills the air,
Secrets held in height,
Love's promise laid bare.

The Dance of Hidden Light

In the dark, a glimmer glows,
A spark concealed from sight,
Mysteries that softly pose,
The dance of hidden light.

Colors twirl in cosmic waves,
Every hue a beat,
In shadows, beauty braves,
A rhythm bittersweet.

Weaving tales of warmth and hope,
In the stillness found,
As galaxies learn to cope,
With silence all around.

The hidden light shines bright,
Amidst the vast unknown,
With each step, the night
Calls us to return home.

Celestial Threads of Fate

In the cosmic weave of time,
Threads of starlight twine,
Every moment a rhyme,
In fate's grand design.

Tales of old and new unfold,
Written in the stars,
In visions yet untold,
We find who we are.

Hands reach across the space,
Tugging at the seams,
Chasing dreams we embrace,
A tapestry of dreams.

With each stitch, we create,
A story we all share,
In celestial threads of fate,
We weave love everywhere.

Celestial Echoes of Ancient Tales

In the stillness of the night,
Whispers of old stories call.
Stars like gems in velvet skies,
Paint the dreams of earth so small.

Galaxies in endless flight,
Carrying tales of times long past.
Echoes of lost civilizations,
In silence, their shadows cast.

Meteors streak with fiery grace,
A reminder of journeys missed.
In the glow of twilight's face,
History's secrets, tightly laced.

The moon, a witness to it all,
Bears the weight of ancient lore.
In every twinkle, truths enthrall,
Celestial echoes forevermore.

When Stars Speak in Secret Tongues

In galaxies far away,
Stars exchange their whispered sighs.
Dancing light on cosmic waves,
Infinite secrets in their eyes.

The night unfolds its velvet shroud,
As constellations weave their tales.
Each twinkle holds a quiet vow,
To guide lost souls through silent gales.

Comets cry with tails aflame,
While planets hum their ancient song.
When stars speak in secret tongues,
Their messages to us belong.

Listen close, the universe sings,
In rhythms soft, yet immensely vast.
Through the void, a harmony rings,
Binding the future with the past.

Unveiling the Astral Veil

Beyond the fabric of the night,
Lies a tapestry of dreams.
Each thread, a star, shining bright,
Unraveling the silent themes.

Nebulas swirl in hues divine,
Painting stories we long to know.
With every pulse and spark that shines,
A mystery waiting to bestow.

Galactic winds send whispers low,
Tales of worlds unseen and rare.
As we gaze, our spirits grow,
In wonder and celestial care.

The astral veil begins to part,
Revealing wonders once concealed.
In the cosmos, we find our heart,
In every ethereal field.

In Search of Forgotten Comets

Through the dark, we chart our way,
In search of comets lost in time.
Their tails like ribbons in the fray,
A celestial dance, pure sublime.

Once bright beacons in the sky,
Now only echoes of their flight.
We seek the trails of days gone by,
To find the sparks that lit the night.

Each celestial wanderer, a tale,
Of journeys vast and wonders grand.
In their paths, we find the frail,
History's brush, a guiding hand.

With stardust dreams, we delve and roam,
Unraveling paths where comets tread.
In search of homes in cosmic chrome,
Where echoes of the past are bred.

Whispers Above the Clouds

Gentle winds caress the skies,
Carrying tales from afar.
Softly they tease and surprise,
In the glow of the evening star.

Echoes of dreams start to blend,
In the hues of dusk's embrace.
Secrets the heavens send,
Drifting in this celestial space.

High above where silence reigns,
Whispers dance among the blue.
Chasing shadows like sweet refrains,
Painting the world with each new view.

Floating joys on cotton wisp,
Moments captured in the air.
Each breath a gentle, tender lisp,
Promising wonders everywhere.

Secrets of Celestial Veils

Through the night, the stars reside,
Guardians of the cosmos' light.
Behind their glow, secrets hide,
Wrapped in dark, mysterious night.

Veils of stardust softly weave,
Patterns of infinity.
In their depths, we long to cleave,
Searching for our destiny.

Constellations tell a tale,
Of love, loss, and dreams fulfilled.
In their paths, we drift like sail,
On the sea of night, distilled.

Celestial whispers linger on,
In the echo of the dawn.
Every heartbeat, every yawn,
Awakens with the sky's new song.

Shadows in the Twilight

As the sun dips low and fades,
Shadows stretch across the ground.
Whispers of the evening wades,
In the cool, embracing sound.

Crickets sing a lullaby,
While the stars begin to gleam.
A canvas painted in the sky,
Awakens every hidden dream.

Time slows in the hush of night,
Secrets gather in the gloom.
Softly shimmers silver light,
Where the shadows find their room.

In the twilight's warm embrace,
Every heart learns to explore.
Finding solace in the space,
Of a world that longs for more.

The Enigma of Distant Stars

Flickering lights in endless night,
Each a story yet untold.
A glimpse of cosmic, wondrous sight,
In their brilliance, we behold.

Time and distance weave their threads,
Connecting dreams from far away.
In the silence, hope embeds,
Guiding us through the darkened sway.

What do they know of our fate?
Do they watch with knowing eyes?
Writing tales we contemplate,
As each moment quickly flies?

Beneath the vast, eternal sphere,
We endeavor to understand.
In the awe, we find our cheer,
United by the stars so grand.

Celestial Legends in Silent Flight

In the vastness of the night,
Stars whisper tales in light,
Ancient dreams take to the sky,
As constellations drift and sigh.

Wings of legends soar so high,
Through the darkness, they comply,
Echoes of those who once roamed,
In the heavens, forever homed.

The moon cradles their lost lore,
While planets keep their secrets stored,
In the silence, stories blend,
As time and space around them bend.

Each flicker holds a spark of flame,
In the cosmos, there's no shame,
For every flight, a tale ignites,
In the dance of silent nights.

Cosmic Secrets in Stellar Light

Underneath the astral dome,
Stars awaken, far from home,
Galaxies with stories to reveal,
Whispers of the cosmos feel.

Nebulas cradle shades untold,
In their depths, the secrets fold,
Comets chase the void with grace,
Leaving trails in time and space.

Each twinkle holds a silent vow,
Of hidden truths that time allows,
In the shimmer of the night,
Cosmic wonders take their flight.

Beyond the grasp of human eyes,
The universe in silence sighs,
Every star, a beacon bright,
Guiding souls through cosmic night.

Celestial Enigmas of the Infinite

In the realm where shadows dance,
Celestial enigmas take their chance,
Infinite paths twist and twine,
In the darkness, stars align.

Questions linger in the night,
As we seek the distant light,
Each constellation a riddle's clasp,
In the void, mysteries gasp.

The echoes of the past collide,
In the cosmos, they abide,
Nebulae weave a cosmic thread,
Binding stories long since dead.

Through the ages, we explore,
Unlocking secrets, seeking more,
In the silence, answers grow,
Beneath the stars' eternal glow.

Beyond the Constellations' Grasp

Beyond the grasp of stars we know,
Lies a realm where wonders flow,
Lost in twilight, mysteries play,
As shadows weave the breaking day.

The Milky Way whispers soft and low,
Guiding dreams where time can't go,
With every flicker, hopes take flight,
In the dance of endless night.

Through the dark, a vision clears,
Each glimmer shines, dissolving fears,
In cosmic tides, we drift and sway,
Finding solace in the fray.

For every star that lights the sky,
Holds a story that will not die,
In the vastness, we belong,
Forever we shall sing our song.

Fragments of Forgotten Stars

Once bright dreams lost in time,
Whispers of light, faded chime.
Scattered pieces roam the night,
Ghostly trails of past delight.

In the dark, they softly glow,
Echoes of what we used to know.
Shattered visions, still they gleam,
Memories caught in a cosmic dream.

They dance along the vast expanse,
A silent waltz, a forgotten chance.
In the stillness of the void,
Beauty in loss, love deployed.

Each fragment tells a story rare,
Of wishes lost and cosmic care.
When we gaze, can we feel?
The warmth of worlds, forever real.

Unwritten Stories of the Starlit Sky

Beneath the twilight's gentle brush,
A canvas waits, quiet, hush.
Stars await our tales to spin,
Secrets held where dreams begin.

Constellations, guides of fate,
Stories linger, yet can't wait.
Every twinkle, a whispered word,
Of moments lost, once unheard.

In the crickets' serenade,
The night's tales, softly laid.
An unwritten book of the skies,
Where hopes and memories rise.

With each glance toward the night,
We find the courage, take flight.
For in the stars' embrace,
Our stories never lose their place.

Hints of Wonder in the Night

Cloaked in shadows, the world does sigh,
In whispers soft, the stars reply.
Each flicker holds a tale untold,
Hints of wonder, bright and bold.

In quiet corners where dreams dwell,
Gleams of magic weave a spell.
Moonlit paths that weave and twist,
Hidden truths in twilight mist.

With every glance, a spark ignites,
Deleting darkness, bringing lights.
The universe, a vast expanse,
Where every star reveals a chance.

Let hearts awaken to the night,
Embrace the glow, feel the light.
For in the stillness, we may find,
The hints of wonder, intertwined.

Ethereal Faces Above Us

Look up, in awe, at the sky's embrace,
Ethereal faces, a spectral trace.
They flicker and dance, alive and free,
Guardians of dreams, in eternity.

With every star, a memory glows,
Of laughter shared and love that flows.
Ancestors watch from celestial heights,
Guiding us through our darkest nights.

Each beam reveals a hidden fate,
In silence, they narrate.
In their gaze, we find our way,
Through the trials of each passing day.

Embrace their light, feel their grace,
These ethereal faces in the cosmic space.
For the night holds more than meets the eye,
A tapestry woven in the sky.

The Infinite Above and Beyond

Stars whisper gently in the night,
Galaxies spiral, a breathtaking sight.
Endless wonders in the cosmic dance,
Eternity beckons, a timeless trance.

Nebulas glow in vibrant hues,
Each twinkle tells tales, old but new.
Comets race across the velvet sky,
In their fleeting paths, dreams defy.

Planets drift in silent grace,
Their orbits a story, a rhythmic pace.
Above and beyond, mysteries unfold,
In the silence, secrets are told.

The universe sparkles, vast and grand,
A canvas of wonders, forever unplanned.
With every glance, we are filled with awe,
Boundless beauty, nature's pure law.

The Arcane Beauty of Heavens

Moonlight bathes the earth in silver,
Gentle shadows, the night does deliver.
Stars like jewels, scattered with care,
Guarding the dreams that float in the air.

Constellations whisper ancient lore,
Mapping the sky, they endlessly soar.
Hidden truths in the dark unfold,
Stories of beauty, timeless and bold.

A celestial dance, planets in line,
Twinkling visions, a sight so divine.
The northern lights, a vibrant display,
Painting the heavens, night turns to day.

In the stillness, the heart finds peace,
From cosmic wonders, troubles release.
Arcane beauty, forever we seek,
In the vastness, our souls softly speak.

Astral Wanderings Under Bated Breath

Footsteps soft upon the midnight dew,
Chasing dreams with the stars as our view.
Hearts flutter as the cosmos calls,
Painting our worries on the galaxy walls.

Under the veil of the velvet night,
Whispers of stardust ignite our flight.
Cosmic threads weave stories untold,
Adventures awaiting, both brave and bold.

Each constellation, a guide on the way,
Illuminating paths where shadows play.
With bated breath, we reach for the skies,
In the astral realm, the spirit flies.

An endless journey, no map to chart,
In stellar whispers, we find our part.
Wanderers lost, yet always found,
In this infinite dance, love knows no bounds.

The Secret Language of Celestial Bodies

In the hush of night, worlds softly speak,
Whispers of light, tender and sleek.
Planets converse in twilight's embrace,
A secret language, a cosmic space.

Comets etch tales across the dark,
Leaving trails of magic, a fleeting spark.
Galaxies beckon with shimmering grace,
In the tapestry woven, they find their place.

Nebulae sigh with colorful dreams,
Painting the air with radiant beams.
Stars blink knowingly, sharing their wisdom,
In the silence, we sense their rhythm.

Dancing in harmony, nature's own song,
A secret language where we all belong.
In the vast expanse, we connect and thrive,
Through celestial whispers, we feel alive.

Where the Horizon Hides

The sun dips low, a golden glow,
Mountains dance in the fading light.
Whispers of dreams in the soft breeze,
Where shadows blend, and day takes flight.

Stars awaken, painting the sky,
A canvas of stories, both old and new.
In twilight's arms, we linger long,
Finding solace where hopes brew.

Time stands still in this sacred space,
As night unfolds its gentle sigh.
In every heartbeat, a promise lies,
Where the horizon meets the eye.

With every wish cast on gleaming stars,
We weave our tales in midnight's embrace.
Where silence sings and dreams collide,
In this realm where the heart finds grace.

Songs of the Nightingale Moon

The nightingale sings to the moon so bright,
A melody soft, in the cool night air.
Stories of love whispered in flight,
Carried by shadows, light as a prayer.

Beneath the branches where secrets dwell,
The stars listen, twinkling in delight.
Each note a echoing, timeless spell,
Enchanting the dark, igniting the night.

The world slows down, wrapped in a dream,
As the nightingale weaves its tender tune.
In every heartbeat, a magic gleam,
Guided by whispers of the silver moon.

With every trill, a promise made,
That in this moment, we are never alone.
For the nightingale sings, unafraid,
Binding our hearts with the moonlight's tone.

The Dance of Wondrous Winds

Winds carry whispers through the tall trees,
A waltz of wonder in the starry night.
They twist and twirl, with such graceful ease,
In a dance of shadows, pure delight.

Across the hills, they sing their song,
Rustling leaves in a tender embrace.
Together they swirl, where spirits belong,
In the realm of dreams, they find their place.

With every gust, a story's told,
Of journey's past and paths anew.
The winds, they never cease to unfold,
Uniting the world in a tapestry true.

As dusk turns to dawn with a gentle sigh,
The dance continues, a never-ending tune.
With every breeze, a chance to fly,
In the arms of the free, beneath the moon.

Beneath the Silver Veil

Beneath the silver veil of night,
The world transforms, wrapped in mystery.
Softly we dream, held in starlight,
Where time surrenders to fantasy.

Midnight's cloak wraps us in bliss,
Every heartbeat whispers a tale.
In quiet corners, magic exists,
Life's fleeting moments shall not fail.

With dreams awakened from gentle sleep,
We wander through this shimmering hue.
For in the silence, promises keep,
And the world reveals its secrets true.

In this realm where shadows play,
We lose ourselves, then find our way.
Beneath the silver veil, we gleam,
Awash in echoes of a dream.

The Veils of Auroral Secrets

Beneath the dawn's embrace, they bloom,
Whispering tales of twilight's loom.
Colors blend in a soft sigh,
Echoing dreams that kiss the sky.

A dance of light on snow's white crest,
Inviting souls to pause and rest.
Secrets spun in threads of gold,
Stirring hearts that yearn to hold.

Each hue a thought, a fleeting chance,
Sketching hope in a fleeting glance.
Veils that shield the world's true face,
Offer glimpses of boundless grace.

In silence, the secrets converge,
Painting skies as colors surge.
Under the auroras' radiant glow,
Hidden stories begin to flow.

Navigating Cosmic Mystique

Stars like pearls in a velvet sea,
Guide the lost on paths yet to be.
Orbits weaving in silent grace,
Mapping journeys through time and space.

Galaxies swirl in a cosmic dance,
Inviting hearts to dream and chance.
Whispers of history softly call,
Encouraging spirits to rise and fall.

Celestial winds stir stardust dreams,
Filling night with twinkling beams.
Each moment a story waiting to wake,
As the universe begins to quake.

Through the void, we drift and sway,
Trusting the stars to light the way.
In the vastness, we find our place,
In cosmic realms of boundless grace.

Secrets Danced in Darkened Skies

Beneath the shroud of night's embrace,
Secrets linger, a hidden trace.
Whispers float on the cool night air,
Echoes of lives once lived with care.

The moonlight weaves a silver thread,
Binding stories of the long dead.
With each flicker of a distant star,
Ancient tales whisper from afar.

In the shadows where dreams reside,
Mysteries tangle, side by side.
A dance unfolds with each bright flare,
Inviting hearts to lay them bare.

Through the night, our spirits glide,
Seeking truths that we can't hide.
In darkened skies, hope is reborn,
As new beginnings chase the morn.

Celestial Keys to the Unknown

Glimmers of wisdom in starlit veins,
Unlocking doors where knowledge reigns.
A universe vast, a canvas wide,
Holds the secrets in time's tide.

Stars like keys to the mysteries show,
Paths unfolding where few dare go.
In the silence, the answers hum,
Inviting hearts to seek and become.

With each pulse of the cosmic light,
A dance emerges in the night.
Every heartbeat sings a song,
Telling us where we all belong.

Beyond the limits of earthly sight,
The cosmos stretches, pure and bright.
In the journey, we learn and know,
The celestial keys to unlock the flow.

Hidden Whispers of the Firmament

In shadows cast by moonlit glow,
Secrets dance in the night's soft flow.
Stars hum gently, a cosmic song,
In whispers hidden, where dreams belong.

Galaxies spin in a silent embrace,
Each twinkle holds a timeless grace.
Mysteries linger, veiled in the dark,
Awakening hearts with a flickering spark.

Celestial voices call from afar,
Guiding the wanderers under the stars.
In the quiet, the universe sighs,
Breathing stories through cosmic skies.

So listen closely, let your heart roam,
Among the wonders, you'll find your home.
In hidden whispers, the truth is unfurled,
A tapestry woven, a starlit world.

Veils of the Celestial Realm

Veils of light adorn the night,
A dance of shades, a beautiful sight.
Clouds of silver, cloaked in dreams,
Hiding secrets in moonlit beams.

The heavens whisper, a sacred tune,
A lullaby sung by the wandering moon.
Stars dressed in shimmering attire,
Light up the cosmos with eternal fire.

Nebulas bloom in vibrant hues,
Painting the dark with emerald views.
Each flicker tells of ages past,
Veiled tales etched in the skies so vast.

In this realm, where time stands still,
Imagination flows, a quiet thrill.
So gaze above, let your spirit soar,
In the celestial dance, forevermore.

The Sky's Forgotten Stories

The sky remembers, the clouds do sigh,
Tales of ages that whisper by.
From ancient realms, the echoes call,
Painting legends on the evening wall.

Winds carry whispers of heroes' fates,
Stories woven through celestial gates.
Each star a memory, a life once lived,
In the cosmic tapestry, love is sieved.

In twilight's embrace, shadows take flight,
Like fleeting dreams in the cloak of night.
Yet forgotten tales linger in the air,
Waiting for hearts that still dare care.

So take a moment, gaze toward the height,
Let the sky share its wisdom and light.
For in these stories of shimmering grace,
Lies the heartbeat of a timeless space.

Stellar Silhouettes

Silhouettes dance in the twilight glow,
Shapes and shadows of worlds we know.
Constellations weave their silent tales,
Guiding the dreamers, like ancient sails.

With every blink, new forms arise,
Crafted from stardust in endless skies.
The cosmos whispers its gentle plea,
To those who dare to dream and see.

Nebulae paint the night's canvas wide,
Where colors meet, and secrets collide.
Each glimpse reveals the universe' art,
Stellar silhouettes that fill the heart.

So look above, let your spirit ignite,
In the grandeur of the cosmic night.
For in those shapes, there lies a key,
To worlds that float in eternity.

A Tapestry of Starlight and Shadows

In the quiet night, stars ignite,
Whispers of dreams, softly taking flight.
Shadows dance beneath the moon's glow,
A tapestry woven in shimmering flow.

Winds carry tales from afar,
Of lovers lost and wishes on a star.
Each twinkle a secret, a story to tell,
In the heart of the night, where fantasies dwell.

The universe spins in a silken thread,
Binding our hopes with the words unsaid.
In this cosmic embrace, we find our way,
A journey through starlight, come what may.

So let us wander where shadows reside,
With starlit dreams as our faithful guide.
For in this dance of night and day,
We are but threads in the cosmic ballet.

The Sky's Hidden Melodies

Above the clouds, a song takes flight,
Melodies hidden in the fabric of light.
With every breeze, a note drifts down,
Whispered secrets from the sky's crown.

The sun hums softly, the moon replies,
Creating harmonies as day complies.
Stars strum chords in the velvet space,
An orchestra hidden, a celestial grace.

In this symphony, we find our peace,
A rhythm of life that will never cease.
In every heartbeat, a tune we learn,
The sky sings on, and we yearn and yearn.

So listen closely, let your spirit soar,
For the sky's hidden melodies call for more.
In the quiet moments, hear the refrain,
Echoing softly like a gentle rain.

Whispers of Time in the Cosmos

Time drifts gently like clouds above,
Each moment a whisper, a fleeting love.
In the vast cosmos, it ebbs and flows,
Secrets of ages, nobody knows.

Galaxies spin in their timeless dance,
Inviting our hearts to take a chance.
In the hush of night, we search the skies,
For the truth of time, where wisdom lies.

The cosmos beckons, a mystery deep,
Holding our dreams in its timeless keep.
We are but echoes in the grand design,
In whispers of time, our souls intertwine.

So let us embrace the fleeting now,
The universe smiles, and yet we bow.
In the silence, find the beauty of fate,
As time waltzes softly, it's never too late.

Constellations of Riddles and Dreams

In the night sky, riddles unfold,
Constellations whisper secrets bold.
Dreams are woven in celestial light,
As starlight dances, a wondrous sight.

Each star a puzzle, a story untold,
A map of the heart, both timid and bold.
In this cosmic vastness, we seek and find,
The answers we cherish, the truths of the mind.

With every glance at the twinkling veil,
We unravel the mysteries where dreams prevail.
In the silence of night, let your hopes soar,
For constellations await, always offering more.

So gaze upon the heavens, let your spirit gleam,
In the constellations of riddles and dreams.
For through the starlit paths, we learn to believe,
In the magic of night, where hearts can weave.

A Journey Through Cosmic Shadows

In the void where silence sings,
Stars collide and darkness clings.
Whispers travel through the mist,
Guided by the cosmic twist.

Nebulae dance, a spectral art,
Painting dreams within the heart.
Galaxies swirl, a timeless race,
Chasing echoes in this space.

With every step, we delve so deep,
Into the shadows, secrets keep.
Time and light begin to bend,
On this journey, there's no end.

The Language of Nightfall

When daylight fades to twilight's grace,
A tranquil hush envelops space.
Stars emerge, a twinkling choir,
Singing softly, never tire.

Moonbeams weave through branches high,
Casting silver on the sky.
Whispers linger in the breeze,
As night unfolds 'neath ancient trees.

Dreams awaken, softly spun,
Underneath the shroud of one.
In this realm, the shadows play,
Crafting tales that fade away.

When Clouds Hold Secrets

Fluffy guardians of the sky,
In their embrace, mysteries lie.
Touching longing, dreams adrift,
They carry whispers, clouds may gift.

Beneath their veil, the sun will beam,
Hiding truths like lost esteem.
In twilight's dance, shadows blend,
Holding secrets, none can send.

A fleeting glance, a wish concealed,
In clouds' embrace, our fates revealed.
Nature's breath in soothing sighs,
Where every hope and sorrow lies.

The Starry Portal to the Unknown

Overhead, the cosmos glows,
Unlocking paths where no one goes.
Asteroids drift, a timeless flow,
A portal where the starlight shows.

Beyond the void, a mystery vast,
Beyond the present, beyond the past.
Nebulae whisper, history spins,
In the silence, the journey begins.

Galactic wonders beckon near,
To the brave, they call with cheer.
Through the portal, we will roam,
The starry skies, our endless home.